In the Small, Small Pond

For David, still the one.

ISBN 0-590-48119-3

 Published by Scholastic Inc., 555 Broadway, New York, NY 10012, by arrangement with Henry Holt and Company, Inc.

19 18 17 2/0

Printed in the U.S.A. 08

First Scholastic printing, September 1994

In the Small, Small Pond

Denise Fleming

SCHOLASTIC INC.
New York Toronto London Auckland Sydney

In the small, small

pond...

wiggle,

jiggle,

tadpoles

wriggle

waddle,

wade,

geese parade

hover,

shiver,

wings quiver

drowse,

doze,

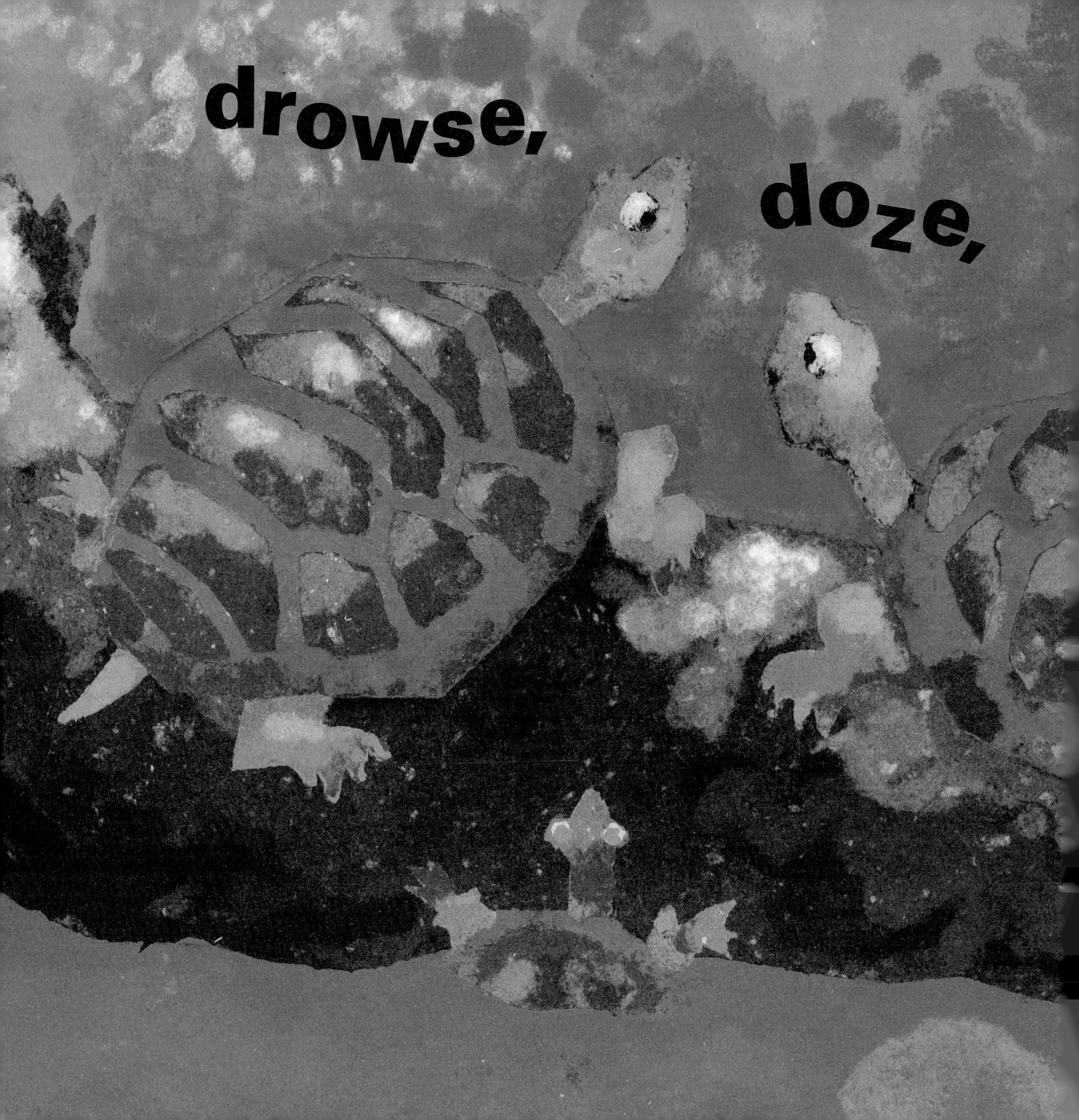

eyes close

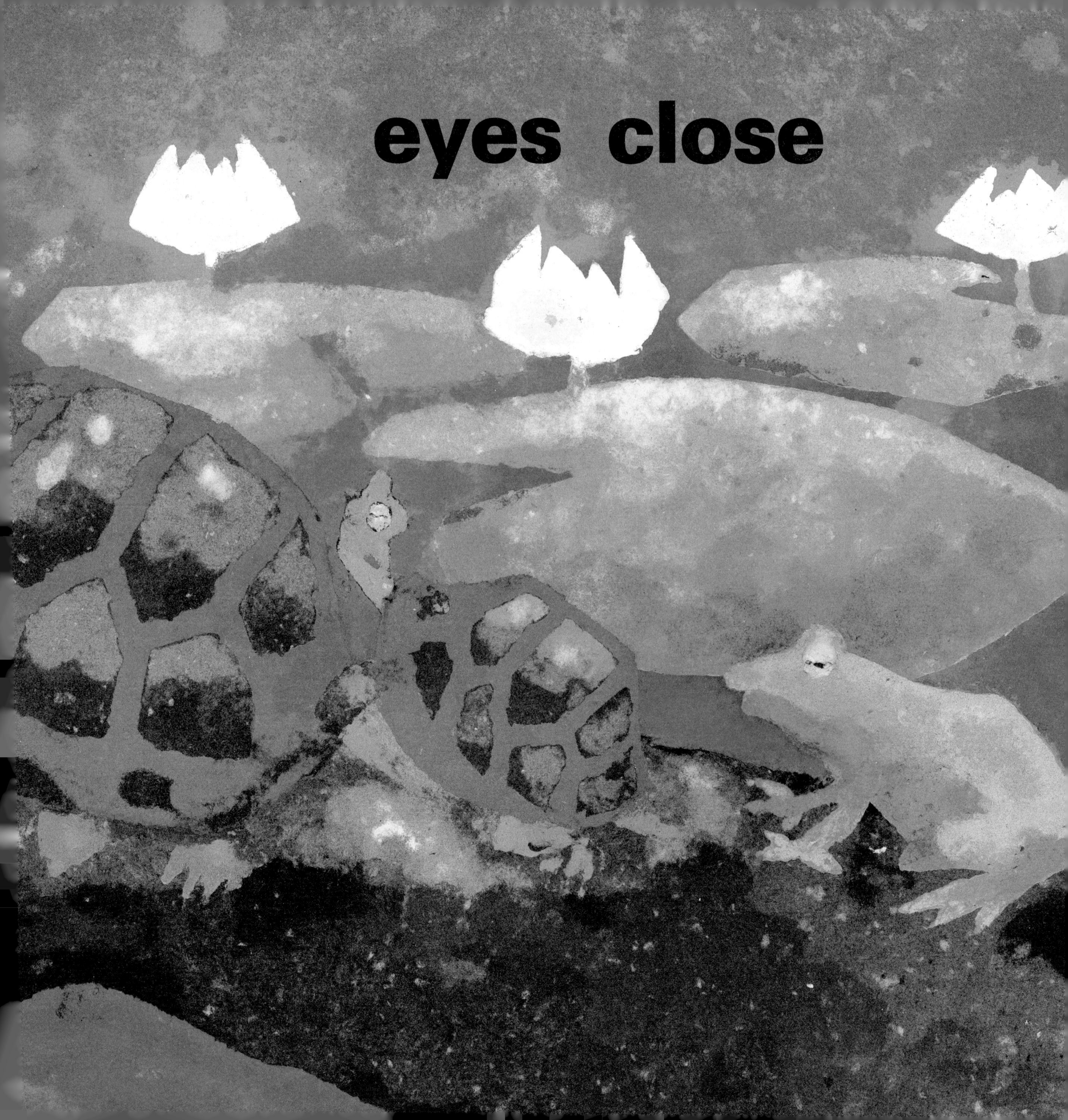

lash,

lunge,

herons plunge

splitter,
splatter,

minnows scatter

circle, swirl,

whirligigs twirl

sweep, swoop,

swallows scoop

click, clack,

claws crack

dabble,

dip,

tails

flip

splish,
splash,
paws flash

pile,
pack,

muskrats
stack.

Chill
breeze,

winter freeze...

cold night,

sleep tight,

small, small

pond.